I0480319

WELCOME TO THE JUNGLE!

Navigating the **Wild** *World of Customer Service*

Jonathan J. Johnson

WELCOME TO THE JUNGLE!
NAVIGATING THE WILD WORLD OF CUSTOMER SERVICE
Copyright © 2019 by Jonathan J. Johnson
ISBN 9781798959138

Designed & Published by King's Daughter Publishing
Indian Trail, North Carolina 28079
www.KingsDaughterPublishing.com

Printed in the United States of America.

DEDICATION

I am grateful to God for creativity and the ability to write. This book would not have come about if it weren't for my time and years of service at Culver's in Belleville, Michigan. Alexis, Brian, Chenea and staff, I am grateful to you for all I've learned and experienced. My hope is that this book will cause you to think and grow as you work in this honorable field of service. ~ Jonathan J. Johnson

TABLE OF CONTENTS

INTRODUCTION

"A man whose name tag read 'Mr. Jonathan' was by far the most polite and awesome drive-thru employee I've ever met. This was probably my second or third time in a VERY long time so I was not familiar with the menu. He began by asking me if this was my first time (I told him what I wrote above) and he then warmly welcomed me back to the jungle and asked me what exactly I was looking to order. I told him that I was very hungry and that I was interested in ordering both chicken tenders and a burger, and he recommended the most affordable and logical options so that I'd be able to order both without over stuffing myself or paying too much money. I went ahead and ordered what he suggested and it turned out great. As I met him at the window, he not only greeted me, but he also greeted my brother who was in the passenger seat. He was great and a perfect example of how ALL customer service employees should be." ~ Guest Comment Card

"WELCOME TO THE JUNGLE!"

This is my signature phrase and how I would generally greet customers when they came in to dine. It was my way of putting a smile on the customer's face and putting them at ease as their eyes widened at the enormous menu from which they had to choose. My name is Mr. Jonathan and I LOVE to make people smile. I get this geeky, goofy feeling when I see people laughing and smiling as a result of my service. It's what I've done practically all my life. No, I am not some guru who has all the powerful wisdom and is pouring it all into this book. I am

7

someone with years of experience dealing with people of all ages—from teaching in the classroom, administrative roles, mentoring and, of course, the years in various customer service arenas, who is sharing what he has learned. I learned through these experiences how to communicate with customers, relate to staff, serve my employers well and be the best of me. This book is simply my way of helping you navigate your way through the "jungle" of being a good customer service agent and growing as a person. This book is a guide to help you as you travel into the wild world of customer service and even beyond.

I am a firm believer in everyone having a village (family, friends, teachers, neighbors, etc.) that will help guide them as they progress on life's journey. As I've continued to grow on my journey, there have been countless conversations and examples set by many of the professionals in my village who have poured into my life. I hope you find the material to be a great resource of knowledge and information. I don't know it all, but what I have learned and know to be true, I share it here with you. With that said, let's get the party started...*WELCOME TO THE JUNGLE!*

CHAPTER 1
THE SAGE GROUSE

Male sage grouse fly to an empty field to dance, strut and puff up their chest to find a mate. The best dancer gets the girl.

In order to get hired, you have to make sure you are an eligible candidate. Do you meet the requirements? Is your resume up to standard? Did you interview well? ARE YOU WILLING AND READY TO WORK? You have to pass the test in these areas in order to be considered employable.

You're out looking for a job.

Maybe you've applied and submitted your resume to many places or have popped into several businesses to see if they were hiring. Let's pause here for a second. If you're going to pop in and check to see if a business is hiring, make sure you present yourself well. I'd get many potential applicants who looked like they just rolled out of bed or came from the club. I beg you to recognize that from the moment you arrive at a business to see if they are hiring, your interview to some degree has begun. The manager that you speak to is already scrutinizing you as to whether you might be a good fit for the business based on how you present yourself at this moment. I'm not saying you have to dress up, but looking presentable to a potential employer makes all the difference with your first impression.

Even if an employer hasn't seen you in person, their first impression of you comes through your resume. The way you fill out your application can cause a hiring manager to move it to the top or bottom of the pile. Submitting a resume with errors like not capitalizing your name, spelling errors, or missing information can also hurt your first impression. If your resume is not sharp (without error and neatly presented), you risk being overlooked for employment. Do yourself a favor. Before you decide to go out to see who's hiring or submit your resume, make sure you are presenting the best version of yourself. You only get one chance to make a first impression. Make it count.

Now if you're like me, or like I was, applying for a position at a restaurant, clothing store or call center was last on my list. Actually, nothing in customer service was even on the list. You might feel like it's beneath you to even apply and internally you are dismissing the idea of serving the public. To that thought process, I respectfully say, "RELAX!" The world of customer service is honorable and you will mature greatly while working in this field. Trust me, I know.

My passion is writing, working with youth and creating new works of art for the stage. But while building that dream, I had to make money. To be honest, I didn't wake up each day excited to put on my uniform and stand for hours on end. But at the end of it all, I appreciate and am grateful for my time working as a server in a restaurant. It gave me a unique chance to utilize my gifts and talents. I got to connect with a range of people and that has impacted my life and my writing. My experience in this world has been like no other and I won't forget it.

Okay, back to you. You now have an interview for a job. Preparation is key. It is important to treat the interview just like you would any other interview. In essence, you need to make sure that you are an eligible candidate for the job. Here are a few things you should remember:

- Have printed, error-free, neat copies of your resume in a folder.

- Read up on the company and learn about their history, culture, and philosophy.
- Get a good night's rest, iron your clothes and take a fresh shower before the interview.
- Show up 10-15 minutes early for your interview.
- Keep cologne/perfume and fragrant lotions to a minimum. You never know who's allergic and you don't want to overpower the interviewer.
- Pop a breath mint/gum before the interview (but get rid of it before going into the interview room).
- Keep your jewelry, make-up, hair and clothing simple.
- Prepare a list of questions to ask in the interview and bring pen and paper to take notes during the interview.
- Turn your cell phone off in an interview.
- Give a firm handshake, maintain eye contact, sit up straight and take time to think before you speak.
- Go into your interview with confidence. Expect to have a great conversation with the interviewer and present yourself as the best candidate for the position.

I shouldn't have to say this, but let me remind you to dress appropriately for the interview. I've interviewed many people whose appearance was disappointing. There were those who came in sandals, shorts, t-shirts and sagging jeans—just completely inappropriate for a professional interview. No, you don't have to come dressed in a suit and bow tie like I did, but a nice pair of slacks, dress shirt or blouse and dress shoes are appropriate.

This is still a professional field and you need to dress professionally for the interview. However, let me say this: not everyone who is preparing for an interview can dress the part. Don't let that discourage you. As an interviewer, I have become sensitive to this fact. My advice is to present yourself as best as you can. If all you have are some Dickies and a button-down shirt, then make sure it looks as clean and neat as possible. A sensitive interviewer should have a heightened awareness to this and should respond appropriately. The point of it all is that you need to be well-prepared for your interview and a well-prepared person gets the job. Now, let's move on and explore your development in the customer service world.

CHAPTER 1: WHOM WOULD YOU HIRE?

Candidate A: Age 28, arrives for his interview exactly on time. He is dressed in jeans that are baggy and drooping, button down shirt (top 2 buttons are open), black sneakers and has many piercings. Candidate A has limited knowledge of the company and can only repeat what he has learned from others or on TV. He has a sketchy work history, which is why he has no resume. Candidate A asks questions focusing on how much money he will earn and how many hours he will work (as he will not work for less than a certain pay and hours). Candidate A has worked six jobs (fired from two and quit the others).

Candidate B: Age 22, arrives 10 minutes early, but an unexpected rush of customers has her waiting an extra 25 minutes before being interviewed. She is dressed in slacks, a sweater, and heels and is prepared with a resume. Candidate B is a bit irritated by having to wait and it shows in her interview. Before the interview begins, she questions how long the interview will take as she has to leave and did not expect to wait so long for the interview. She arrogantly shares her knowledge of the company proving she's informed and "knows how to interview." She asks questions mainly about management as she is only interested in a leadership position, believing her experience proves she should be in management. She fidgets during the interview and checks her watch several times. Her lack of focus causes the interviewer to thank her for her time and cut the interview short.

Candidate C: Age 19, arrives 5 minutes late for the interview and pleads for forgiveness as his bus was running late. He is dressed in wrinkled cargo pants with a small hole in the knee, a button down shirt and worn sneakers. He proves in the interview that he has learned about the company and has many questions about what his job may entail. Candidate C has limited work experience and is in need of a job. He is eager and willing to learn and do whatever the job requires of him. He shakes hands with the interviewer and thanks them for their time.

- *Whom would you hire? Why or why not?*

- *What mistakes do you see in each candidate's interview?*

- *What positives do you see in each candidate's interview?*

CHAPTER 2
THE CHEETAH

Cheetahs spend two years in isolation with their mother developing themselves, their knowledge of the land, and their hunting and survival skills.

The process of developing and strengthening your character is a powerful process, but it's necessary for your growth. Working in customer service opened my eyes to some of my weak areas and provided me with plenty of opportunities to grow. You have a lot of learning to do about yourself, your new team and the lay of the land. Let's take a look at how to develop YOU!

YOU ARE HIRED! NOW WHAT?

You Are Here.

It's time to work. There will be days when you feel really great about your job and there will be days you might not feel as great. People will demean the work you do. There will be snide remarks. You may feel "some kinda way" about wearing your uniform and all those factors can affect you. Don't let your emotions get the best of you. You are here. You have a job after a long search for employment. You are doing honorable work and receiving payment for your work. This is life for you now. Embrace it, own it and live it to the fullest.

WORKPLACE 101

Be You

You were hired because you were able to articulate who you are and your qualifications in the interview process better than others. It was more than having good answers...it was YOU! Your personality, charm and charisma came shining through and that's why you were hired. Being you in all of your serious, creative, kooky, talkative, friendly ways is what will cause you to have favor with your manager, develop relationships with your co-workers and make positive, influential connections with the customers. You must be yourself.

When I interviewed for my job, I arrived in a suit and bow tie/handkerchief combo and yeah, it might have been overkill, but that's me. I was the only one of my co-workers hired on the spot. At first I was seen as the weird guy on staff. My personal style and charisma is a bit overwhelming and my co-workers didn't quite relate. Yet, the more I was just me, the easier it became to converse with my co-workers and even set a standard among them. Eventually, I was able to relate better to the staff as different ones tried to impersonate me in my interactions with the guests. They say imitation is the sincerest form of flattery and my co-workers tried to imitate me a lot, which was pretty cool.

You being you is going to make a difference in the workplace. I can attest to it. Be bold enough to stand out and watch how you will be rewarded and respected as a result of it.

Get Off Your Throne

It was extremely frustrating and tiresome to work with people who acted like they were too good to do the work. When I first started on the job, I closed the restaurant several nights a week and always had to clean the dining room and the bathrooms. I hated it, but I quickly developed a rhythm and closing became less of a chore. I learned how to do my job and do it right.

Frustration would set in when others on staff acted in disbelief when they were asked to help with cleaning responsibilities. One young lady would begin to cry when asked, but she had to do her job. Everyone, including the owner, did all kinds of cleaning chores. There was no exception. We all worked to make the place run as smoothly and effectively as possible. When you get a job, you have no right to say what you will and will not do. Whatever your manager asks you to do, do it well. You are not at home and don't have someone to clean up the mess. In the workplace you are not royalty. You don't have to like it, but your job is to complete a task. Get it done.

You Must Have Patience

There is a lot to learn when you enter the job. You are expected to fully grasp the language, culture, speed, and systems in a relatively short time span. It's unfair to a degree, but you can't pressure yourself to learn any faster than your natural speed. You will fumble all over the place with mistakes trying to prove that you know what to do when you don't. You have a learning curve and you must be patient with your learning curve, but that doesn't mean you can't challenge yourself.

You also must study, learn and practice everything you've read or have been taught on and off the job. Your first couple of weeks on the job should be spent becoming proficient in how to do your work, not trying to become popular with your co-workers. There will be time for that later. While you're at work, take every advantage to test your knowledge in every area. Ask as many questions as needed. Keep a small notepad and pen with you to take notes on what you've learned from the day and what areas you need to improve. Then go home and study. Come back the next day with a better degree of knowledge and focus. You never know what kind of pop quizzes your manager may spring on you just to see how well you're learning!

Patience is a virtue you will need to have and carry every day. You will need to have patience with your co-workers when they don't hustle as hard as you or have a bad attitude. You will need to have patience with your managers when they micromanage you or overly critique your work. You will need to have patience with the customers when they are rude or demanding. You may find this subject addressed in your performance/raise evaluations, so it's important to work on it. Patience is something that you must encourage yourself to have at all times on the job. It will be tested with yourself and others.

Stay Sharp

While at work, your focus game has to be sharp. You need to be aware of what's going on in the environment. Pay attention to the notes your manager gives you at the beginning of your shift (items out of stock, issues in the store, promotional items, etc.). Pay attention to the needs of the staff. If someone is not feeling well or having a bad day, your energy may need to increase in order to help the flow of the shift. Pay attention to the customers and their needs. There might be a customer with a question or who might need assistance in some other way. If you are distracted in any way, you might find yourself ineffective during that shift and your co-workers/customers do not need help from an unfocused person. Whatever the moment, give each shift your ultimate focus.

The truth is, you will come to work with all sorts of thoughts on your mind and things going on in your life. You have to check your personal life at the door and be prepared to give of yourself 100% while at work. It's not about you.

I have to be honest. As a writer, I can easily daydream or get caught up in my creativity. At times, my thoughts caused me to be distracted and that's something I had to monitor. I learned how to keep a notepad with me and when I had a thought, I would write it down quickly and revisit it when I got home from work. That simple act helped me to be more focused at work, yet also provided a way for me to explore my thoughts without getting lost in them.

Being alert is essential for any employee. With all the things we have going on in life, it's easy sometimes to go on auto-pilot and mentally check out.

You have a job to do. Everyone needs your focus and attention. Focus your focus.

Learn Your Customer Service Voice and Language

You have an authentic customer service voice. It's important that you understand this and develop it. It's important to speak the language of your professional environment. Just like you have language you speak around your friends, family, or at school, the same goes for the work environment. I use a friendly respectful greeting with customers such as, "Welcome, my lady" or "Have a great day, kind sir." There's a few "How you doing, my friend?" in the mix, but that's my vibe with the customers. I know I sound like somebody from the olden days, but that's how I do things and the customers respond to me. I know my customer service voice and language. Now you need to know and learn yours.

As you learn your voice, you will begin to learn the art of communicating with people of all ages and educational, socioeconomic and cultural backgrounds. You will have opportunities to engage the customer further and you should take advantage of every opportunity. Customers will come in with all kinds of humor and craziness and you will need to know how to interact with them. How you talk to the elderly, or a big family, or a group of business executives will vary. Each culture of people has a vibe and you need to pick up on that vibe in order to communicate with them effectively. The more you engage customers, the more you learn about yourself and expand your customer service language skills.

In addition, I challenge you to learn the value of positive communication. Think of yourself as a customer: how did you feel when a worker told you haphazardly that they were out of a product and then abruptly walked away? It would behoove you to learn how to sweeten your responses. Instead of "Oh, we're out of that." Try, "I'm sorry that item is out of stock, but we should have a shipment in on Friday." Simply learning to add a little "sugar" to your response will make for better interactions with customers and prompts them to return for your service because of how respectfully you speak to them. Developing your customer service language and voice distinguishes you and teaches the customer what kind of experience they can expect from you. Don't take it lightly. It's important.

Have Integrity and Character

Trust me when I say that having integrity and character is important not just for work, but for your overall life's journey. People need to be able to trust you, your word and your work ethic. When you were hired, immediately a trust was graced upon you. It is assumed and believed that you won't lie, steal or show up late for work. You were hired with the belief that you will be a model employee. Yet, if you don't have integrity or even care about your integrity, you will not survive as an employee–anywhere. Your employer is watching you and checking you out at all times to make sure that you are a trusted employee. I guarantee you, your manager is internally asking themselves questions like:

- Is this employee supporting, protecting and upholding the image of the company?
- Do they break any rules?
- Are they a good representative of the company in their words and actions?
- Are they a supportive co-worker or do they gossip about everybody?
- Do they shortcut their work or do they follow protocol?

Your character and integrity are what can make or break you. Your manager is watching you to see if they made the right choice in hiring you. Customers are looking for a solid employee who will handle their needs with care and concern. You want to be a stand up person in and out of the work environment.

On the other hand, integrity doesn't just stop inside the work environment. In this day and age of social media, you might become friends with your co-workers and maybe even customers in various social media worlds. Make sure that what you are posting is in line with your character. You don't want to be one person at work and then a different person on social media. I am a man who is a Christian, black, an actor, singer and has a quirky sense of humor. That's who you will get when you interact with me in the workplace and in the social media world. I'm Jonathan at all times and that's what has allowed me to receive several commendations, raises, and promotions all because I know who I am and live that out every moment of my life. Having strong character and integrity will cause you to have favor and open doors for you both in and outside of the workplace.

Mind Your Manners

When it comes to respect, I always say "Sir/Madam," "please and thank you," or "excuse me/pardon me." I use that language as a sign of respect and not familiarity as I would use with my friends and family. Replying to a person with "What?!" can be disrespectful. I would watch many co-workers use that phrase and its tone would ruffle feathers. Manners seem to be a lost art. It is still good practice to open doors for others, help the elderly, and greet people. My grandmother instilled in me the golden rule: "Do unto others as you would have them do unto you." It is just plain respectful to respond to your manager, co-workers and customers with a positive tone when communicating with them. They are not your friends from your neighborhood and should not be addressed in a familiar manner. Check out the list below of some healthy ways to respond to others:

- Yes Sir/No Sir
- Excuse me
- I beg your pardon
- I'm sorry, can you repeat that?
- Thank you/You're welcome
- Have a great day!

Incorporating phrases like these into your work language (even everyday language) will take you far and make relating to others better. It will also help to eliminate the "Huh?" or "What did you say?" from your vocabulary. Watch how manners will help to change your environment.

Get Over Yourself

I used to work with a woman who was on the kitchen crew. At any moment, we could get a mad rush of customers and since she worked the fryers she may have to drop multiple pieces of chicken or fish. Without fail, she would blow-up and get overly frustrated when she knew this is how things worked. It was as if she was surprised that we were getting business and that would cause her to become outraged every time big orders rolled in. It was frustrating many days to work with her because her attitude would affect the entire staff. You don't want to be that person.

When you are at work, it is *sooooo* not about you. You are a part of a team and everyone needs you to pull your weight in order to ensure the success of that shift. Everyone is going to have days where they don't feel well, their personal life is in disarray or life just seems unfair. Your work can suffer if you have a bad attitude or if your focus is on your problems.

You'll make mistakes, ignore responsibilities and might find yourself not caring about the quality of your work. Everyone suffers with an attitude like this on occasion. You can deal with whatever you need to deal with after your shift. Right now, you need to help the team and give great service to the customers. There is no room for negative energy.

On the other hand, remember that you are not perfect and you will make mistakes. Correction is a part of the process. It sucks to work with someone who has a "know it all" attitude. You will be corrected by your leaders or team members if you perform incorrect procedures, don't use the proper company language, forget to do something or don't smile. Accept it, fix it and get over yourself.

It's not about you.

WELCOME TO THE JUNGLE!

ESSENTIAL SKILLS

Be Able to "Code Switch"

Here's the thing. If you didn't know it, there are several sides to you. I don't care how much of a laid-back person you might be, you are not one-sided. You have to learn how to bring out which element of you is needed for any given situation (school, church, interview, wedding, etc.). Maybe you haven't fully developed your professional side, but entering the world of customer service will teach you how to do so.

If you want to make it in this world and maintain your job, you're going to have to be able to "code switch." This simply means allowing the other aspects of who you are to operate when needed. It does not mean trying to act like someone or something else. Let me give you an example.

In my world, I have to be able to communicate with theatre artists, singers, church members, high school students, as well as family and friends. Each culture has its own vibe and language and I'm expected to know how to immerse myself in each world. However, as a server, I was able to maintain a level of professionalism and speak to each of these cultures whenever they came into the restaurant. I didn't have to plaster a fake smile or fake welcome. If I recognized a certain vibe of a person, I maintained the integrity of the role of my job, but communicated with them in way that was comfortable for them to understand the process of ordering. The same goes for you. There's a certain language and relationship you will need to learn when it comes to dealing with your manager, customers and co-workers. You will have to get comfortable engaging the public in various ways. Where you might have been able to act shy before, now you have to be in the face of the people and have high energy.

This world will require much of you and if you are not willing to learn how to operate fully in it, you will not make it. You're not being fake, you're being you on another level.

Be Confident

You will encounter a range of scenarios that will try to challenge your self-esteem, your knowledge of the business and your integrity. You must have confidence in all you do. Customers will be impatient, co-workers will try to outshine you and your manager may get frustrated with you and try to challenge your work ethic. You can't be shaken by the energy of others. You've got to stay strong in who you are, what you know and what you can do. Confidence is everything and it's what you'll need to survive in this industry.

Be Able to Work Under Pressure

Each area of customer service has its own level of intensity. In the fast food world, you have to deal with various kinds of rush crowds, kids nights, coupon madness, etc. In the retail world, you'll have various kinds of sales and hot new items which will bring a crowd and that will be challenging. Regardless of the environment, you need to learn how to handle the pressure. You'll find that co-workers, customers and even your manager can become pretty intense in strenuous situations. That doesn't mean you have to be like them. Learn how to be calm in the midst of a storm. You can be the rational, quick thinking and peaceful presence needed to keep the positive energy in the place. Let your cool spirit prevail. Maintain your peace.

Be Flexible

Flexibility is key. There were many days I would come in to work early to get some writing done, only to be interrupted and have to jump in and help. There were days I was tired and ready to get off my shift and had to stay longer to help through a sudden rush. I had to be a team player. You will have to do the same. There will be times when you will be needed to come in early, stay late, cover a shift or help in other ways. Yeah, it does kind of suck when you're always the one being flexible, but watch how it can and will benefit you in future situations. Don't be the person who is so focused on working their shift that they overwhelm the manager with questions like, "Am I done?" or "Can I go?"

I used to get really irritated and frustrated with the workers who would work a few short hours and then question endlessly if they could go home while they saw me running around trying to complete orders or handle matters in the store. They were very impatient and didn't care that business was being handled. They just wanted to go home. I challenge you to be the kind of employee who can be depended upon to be a team player and not look out for themselves only.

Be Aware of the Basics

We all need help sometimes with being aware of things. Now, this isn't a comprehensive list, but here are some simple things to be aware of:

- Open doors for your guests, especially the elderly, disabled or mothers with strollers. It's a common courtesy and your guests will appreciate it.
- Wash your hands OFTEN! When you sweep, take out the trash, pick up trash off the floor, scratch your arms, twirl your hair or whatever you do, simply wash your hands. It is a given in customer service interaction. You are likely to shake hands with someone or maybe even give someone a hug and you don't want to spread germs or any kind of nastiness. Customers will wait for service from someone with clean hands.
- Make sure your uniform is clean and neat. Take the time to look presentable.
- Pick up after yourself.
- Come to work on time. Early is always best and call if you will be late.
- Speak to the customers. Say "Hi."

Get it. The simple stuff.

Professional Etiquette

Regardless of your age, you are now a professional. This means family and friends become customers when they enter the store. Friends and family will come by and want to socialize, get a discount or mess with you on the job. Your manager and co-workers are watching you to see how you will deal with these kinds of situations. You have to remind your loved ones that they should only come in to see you for business purposes and keep personal matters to when you're off the clock.

Beyond that, if you are really good at your job, you might find yourself being pursued by other employers who might be patronizing your business. They will watch how you handle servicing them and become impressed. That's a good thing. However, you have to be cautious with these kinds of people. They might pull you to the side and hand you a business card or inform you they want to hire you. You might be flattered and that's cool, but you are still at work. My advice is to minimize conversation as much as possible so your manager doesn't get offended by you talking to potential employer. Quickly write down your information and ask them to contact you offline and then get back to work. I've been in that scenario many times and I had to make sure not to conduct that kind of business while at work. I'd kindly take their card or give them my info and move on with my business. It might happen, just maintain your professionalism.

A side note to parents of teenagers: Let your child be a professional. In the workplace, you are not Mom and Dad. You need to teach your child about their responsibilities. If they need time off for a family function or doctor's appointment, then you should give them that information well in advance so they can request the day off. You cannot come up to the job and get in the manager's face because your child's schedule conflicts with your plans. Does anyone do that for you on your job? NO! You're interfering with your child's work, which can hurt them and cause them to be disciplined or even experience the loss of a job. Teach your child how to read their schedule, to be mindful of time off requests and any other information they need to know. Then let them handle their own business. They are going to have to learn how to make decisions and handle responsibility. Isn't that why you made them get a job to begin with?

Goal-Oriented

What is your focus as you take on this job? Are you just concerned about a paycheck or do you desire to grow? Goals and ambitions are necessary for whatever you do in life. If you only took the job just to pay the bills, I get it. However, let me challenge you. Have you thought about aspiring to get out of debt, saving some money to travel, or purchasing some new items for yourself? Don't just work to get by. Work to put yourself in a position to have more, in order to do and be more.

It is also good to set daily, weekly and monthly goals. Make a plan for becoming self-sufficient on the register, having full knowledge of the inner workings of the store, being able to do other tasks without assistance and so on. It's more than just coming to work. Having goals keeps you focused on your tasks and what you need to know for your job. It also shows your manager how hard a worker you are and that you are more than just an average employee.

My daily goal was to grow to become a better person. I worked hard to establish good relationships with the crew, positive interactions with the customers and did my best to lead by example in all I said or did. Setting goals is part of life's journey, so it's good to incorporate goal planning into all you do. It makes a big difference in how you handle yourself on the job and in life.

Well, we've talked a lot about you, now let's explore developing relationships with others in the workplace.

BE A LEADER

Leadership Track

In the world of customer service, there are ways to progress and grow. You cannot set your sights on becoming a manager or higher, if you don't understand or respect the progression of leadership.

There is a developmental process and you have to understand that each level will have added responsibility. If you want to advance in leadership positions, learn from and talk to other leaders in those positions. Get tips from them on what they did to gain the promotion and what is required of that position. Become knowledgeable about what you need to do get to the next level.

Your mantra should be, "Do as I do, not do as I say." Your crew should follow your leadership example, not be led by a dictator.

Be prepared to be challenged. Not everyone will celebrate your progression and some may even challenge your leadership and authority.

Be prepared to lose friends. Those who you thought were in your corner might become jealous of you and resent you telling them what to do. It comes with the territory.

Be ready for more: leadership meetings, reports, classes, longer/extra shifts. A lot more is going to be required of you. "To whom much is given, much is required."

Be ready to make critical and on the spot decisions. You will have to deal with machines breaking down, problems with customers, running out of stock of certain items in the middle of a shift and more. As a leader, you will have to learn how to deal with those problems on the spot and continue to lead the crew through the shift.

Just stay strong and focused. Growing to become a leader is going to strengthen and make a better you.

CHAPTER 2:
WHAT WOULD
YOU DO?

Scenario 1: It's your first weekend with two other new hires. You struggle with the register and keeping up with the fast pace, whereas the other new hires have no trouble. Your manager uses you to run orders, clean-up bathrooms and get products from storage. You feel dejected and think you are doing a bad job. How do you handle your emotions? How do you deal with your perceived thoughts about your first day, co-workers and manager? How do you overcome your trouble with the registers and quick-paced environment?

Scenario 2: A bus of 60 teenagers and staff arrives and fills the lobby. Business is already booming and the staff becomes overwhelmed. Your manager has to jump in to help in other areas and leaves you and the rest of the crew to man the front. With your skill set, how can you aid the situation? How can you motivate the staff?

Scenario 3: You notice your co-worker has not completed all of their tasks and just clocked out and left. Your manager sees things left undone and questions what happens. Do you blame your co-worker? Do you offer to finish the task even though it's not your responsibility? How could you make this situation better?

CHAPTER 3
THE ELEPHANT

Elephants are identifiable by their long trunks, big ears, white tusks and their pillar-like legs. They are known to be friendly, but will trample when mad or scared.

There are elements in life that will identify you, such as the familiarity of your family name, your friends, or the various social groups to which you belong. They all make up your identity. When you get hired into a new position, you are now a part of a brand. You have a new identity to embrace. You have a responsibility to live up to the company's standards, practices, and culture and serve to promote the brand in a healthy manner.

Here's what you have to understand. You were hired not only because it was believed that you could handle the elements of the job, but also that you would be a great ambassador of the brand. You will be expected to embrace the culture, know the brand and be able to articulate the brand to any and everyone. Let's explore.

Embracing the Culture

Every company has a culture and a focus that sets the atmosphere for the business. Some companies are family-oriented, while others might be fast paced and geared towards handling as many transactions as possible. There are companies with more relaxed atmospheres, and others centered around structure and organization. Whatever the culture is, you have to embrace it. The culture has to become a part of how you operate and move in the workplace. As you embrace the culture, it will be evident in all of your work practices. Embracing the culture is not about whether you agree or disagree with it, but it's about you honoring the atmosphere of the business in all you say and do. When you don't honor the brand, it can send mixed messages to customers and even your co-workers (the ones who may be following your example). You want to make sure to set an example that everyone will follow and respect.

Know the Brand

What company do you work for? What is their history? What are they known for? These are some of the many questions you should be asking when you become an employee. As a representative of the company, you may be faced with these kinds of questions from customers and people who have little knowledge about the business. You should feel comfortable answering these kinds of questions both in and outside of work. You become the first teacher for the customer. Customers will come in thinking they know what's going on, but you can help them with an intimate knowledge of how things work.

For instance, I would serve customers who would order a deluxe burger which generally comes with onions, pickles, mayo, lettuce, tomato and American cheese. I would always shock them by asking them what kind of cheese they wanted (American, cheddar, swiss or a combo), if they wanted grilled onions instead of raw, or if they wanted to shake up the burger by adding BBQ sauce or bacon. Customers appreciated this gesture, as most never realized they had options when it came to building their perfect burger.

The more intimate I became with the brand and its inner workings, I was better able to offer more options to the customers. The result would be customers returning and feeling more confident and knowledgeable with their ordering as a result of their lesson with me. Understanding the brand and being able to articulate it to others, proves you to be more than just an average employee. You never know what kind of opportunities, promotions or experiences could happen as a result of you going the extra mile to gain and utilize this kind of knowledge. Take the initiative to become an expert.

Articulate the Brand

Every company has its own language. For instance, an ice cream dessert with toppings mixed into it might be known as a "blizzard" at one company, a "flurry" at another and a "mixer" at a different company. It's the same dessert with three different names, but each name is signature to that company. Your job is to learn the language that is signature of the company where you work. As you learn the language, you have to incorporate it in all you do. As you speak the language, you are better able to communicate with co-workers and educate the customers on how to utilize the language in conducting their business. Customers are prone to get frustrated when they are trying to transact business and they are speaking one language and you are speaking another.

Your job is to have a handle of the language. This helps when you have to interpret what the customer thinks they are saying, and in return, you have an opportunity to teach them the right language. At my restaurant, we used the words "short, medium and tall" for dessert drinks and often in the drive-thru it would get misinterpreted when a customer ordered a "small" and it was rung up as a "tall." Those kind of mistakes were costly. So to clarify, we would ask, "Is that a short, medium or tall?" to make sure we understood the size and also teach the customer that this is the language you need to use when ordering a dessert drink. Teaching the customer the language should be a polite and respectful interaction. You want them to learn and not get mad at you for being rude or disrespectful. As you talk the talk, you'll help others do so as well.

CHAPTER 3: WHAT WOULD YOU DO?

Scenario 1: You overhear your co-worker and a customer having a frustrating encounter. The customer is trying to communicate their needs for their purchase, but uses language unfamiliar to your co-worker. You sense how to help the customer and resolve the situation. How can you aid in this matter with sensitivity and respect to both your co-worker and the customer? How can you help teach the customer the language they need to use in order to conduct effective business in the future?

Scenario 2: You encounter a co-worker who constantly uses the wrong language that doesn't promote or articulate the brand. This co-worker's lack of learning the language has caused problems with customers' orders to the point where management has had to refund money for purchases and the store has received negative reviews. You sense your manager is getting ready to fire this co-worker. Do you try to help your co-worker get better at their job? Do you let them know they are about to be fired? Should you do anything at all?

Scenario 3: Your manager chooses you to be part of a team to represent the company at a community fair. They instruct that you will have literature and business cards to pass out while engaging with the public. You will serve as the face of the company and representative for your location. How do you prepare yourself for such an opportunity? Do you feel versed in the knowledge and language of the company? Can you articulate the brand with ease and clarity?

CHAPTER 4
THE LION

A king doesn't need to be perfect. He just needs to own his role as leader who has authority.

It might sound weird, but developing a relationship with your employer/manager is essential. I have had some pretty amazing employers over the years, and with all of them, I was able to connect on a deeper level. I had one manager who was sensitive to the strenuous nature of the job. He had an open door invitation to his house to the staff to relax, play games, hold meetings and eat. There was one who was an extreme giver, so it wasn't uncommon for her to surprise the staff with lunch, snacks or spontaneous car rides to chat while grabbing a sweet treat. Whatever the connection, I cherished the relationships I was able to establish with my former leaders, as it allowed me to gain a better understanding of them and it helped me be a better employee under their leadership.

Think about it: your manager hires you, promotes you, decides your raise and evaluations, and will be the one to recommend you whenever you decide to move on from the job. While you don't develop a relationship with your manager to get favors or special treatment, this is a chance for you to both understand and relate to each other. Think of the advantage you'll have if you learn the telltale signs of worry, frustration, happiness or anger in your manager. You'll know how to respond in each of these situations and can help your co-workers with how they should respond as well.

Thinking in a bigger picture, as your leaders understand the truth of your character, you'll never know how they will begin to utilize you in the workplace. There are always opportunities for team leadership, community engagements, administrative tasks and more. Your manager is always looking for someone to fill these voids and if they know and trust your character, you will be a likely candidate. Let's explore developing a strong relationship with your boss.

Be a Person of Your Word

In the interview process, you probably made a lot of statements to upsell your skills to the interviewer. You made sure you came across in the best light so that you would land the job. You probably said something like, "Oh yes, I am a very outgoing person and love to talk to people. I have great energy and will be very energetic on the job." I get it. At times, I've said what I thought should be said to get the job. Yet, now that you have the job, your manager is looking for that person you talked about in the interview to show up to work. Now you have to make good on your word. It goes beyond just showing up on time and punching a time clock.

Your manager needs to see from the beginning, the energetic people person you said you were. That's who they need to see working and connecting with customers. You sold your personality in the interview and you can't afford not to be that person. At the end of the day, whoever you say you are, whatever you say you'll do, make sure it's the truth and stand on your word.

Go the Extra Mile

As one who's been in management, I really appreciated the workers who didn't have to be told every single thing to do. I liked to work with the ones who knew the elements of the shift and got the job done. There are many managers who are the same way. You should never be one who needs to be told every single thing to do on a shift. Each shift has its own rhythm and pace. It's your job to learn quickly how the various shifts run, so you'll know what to do whenever you are scheduled. When working, if you see a need, fill it. Don't look for a pat on the back for everything you do. You're not a little kid. A mature person knows how to step up when it's time. Take advantage of opportunities to do more and be more (especially when your co-workers aren't trying). Trust that when you do more, it is being noted and will not be forgotten.

Go farther. Do more.

Respect Your Leader

I've had many conversations with employees about their lack of respect toward me (or another manager) and that it needed to cease. That usually brought a change in their attitude, but those conversations made me take note for this particular section. Respect should be given regardless of how you feel about a person.

Each manager is different. Some will be more laid back, some will be strictly by the book and others will try to be everybody's friend. The fact is, regardless of the manager you are working with on any shift, you need to have respect for that manager and their leadership style. You don't have to like it, but you do have to respect it. Your job is to learn the leadership style of each of your managers, so when you have to work with them you know what they expect of you. Don't you dare utter the words "Well _____ does it this way" or "That's not how _____ does it." Those statements are null and void as each manager is going to lead their shift according to how they see fit and you have to follow suit.

If you want your manager to respect you and what you can do, then you have to help them see and understand your talents by simply doing your work. They will be more likely to give you latitude if you simply do your job well. Work to understand and respect these various styles of leadership. It will cause a more positive work atmosphere and will establish a better bond between manager and employee.

SHHHH!

It was really annoying and frustrating when I would watch crew members get snippy with the supervisor in charge (including me) or try to usurp their authority. If they call you to do something, your job is to simply comply. You should never combat or argue with your manager in front of other employees or customers. There might be a lot of needs on a shift and many people will try to pull you in different directions, but the only voice you should be acutely aware of is your manager. The directives they give trump any other voice. If you are confused about direction, then you can politely ask your manager, "I was given instruction to clean up that spill. Should I do that or what you are telling me to do?" Then let them clarify for you the order of how you should finish your tasks. Don't just get frustrated with them and blow up in front of everybody. If you're not going to respectfully ask for clarification, then your only response is to *"shhhhh."*

This can be especially tough when it comes to co-managers. I once watched one of the "shift managers" question the general manager in front of a customer because they disagreed with her decision. I couldn't believe my eyes when I saw it take place because it was done in front of a guest and a crew member. If you have questions or misunderstandings about your manager's decisions, then you should politely and respectfully talk with them offline and not in front of the others. Respect should be given to all because you are going to want respect back when it's your turn to lead. Get it? Got it? Good!

Stop Talking So Much

As you get to know your supervisor, it's easy to fall into the notion that you've become friends. Your supervisor is not your friend and is not required to be keeper of all your secrets. You should be careful what and how you share personal information with your manager. Don't get catty and share gossip. Remember, maintaining a relationship with your supervisor is about honoring and respecting them as your leader, all the while maintaining the sanctity of the bond you have established with them. Keep conversations with your supervisor healthy and professional at all times. It's the best way.

Don't Combat. Resolve.

I have to say one of the things that was/is most frustrating about workers today, is that many don't know how to deal with conflict. I would watch co-workers carry their frustrations around until they started to blow off steam with snide comments toward their manager and things would blow-up in a heated argument. Becoming snarky, rude or combative is not the way to handle an argument. It's sad that some people do not know how to deal with their issues.

Differences are bound to happen between people, but how you handle differences with your manager is important. Your manager may get on your nerves with their demanding tone or nitpicking of your work, but it is never an excuse to lash out at them. That is a sure sign of immaturity. So, how do you handle disagreements, frustrations or anger at your manager (this can apply to anyone)?

DO NOT argue with your supervisor openly in front of your co-workers and customers. You're the one who will look like a fool. Shut your mouth. Bite your tongue. Walk away from the situation and cool down. Take a moment to clear your head before going back to work. A clear, cool head allows for you to address the situation privately and civilly. Now, although I believe face-to-face conversations are best, if you have to, you can use the phone or email to address the problem. Taking your business out of the public allows for both parties to clear the air without the prying eyes/ears of others. Handling your frustrations publicly is always bad for you and for business. No one needs that.

DO NOT address an issue out of anger, frustration, cockiness or bitterness. Those kinds of emotions can/will cloud your judgement and will ensure for an unsuccessful resolution. It's best to address an issue when your motives are pure in spirit and your mind is calm. Make sure to come with an open mind to resolve things in a healthy manner.

DO NOT set out to prove your point. It shouldn't be about proving that you were right or making your manager look bad. That's childish. It's not all about you or your bruised ego. You should try to resolve an issue so that understanding will prevail, not that you will be proven right.

DO understand that just because you're ready to resolve things, your manager may not be. Be flexible and give the other party the grace and space to talk when they are ready. Nothing gets resolved unless both parties are in a peaceful frame of mind to find resolution.

DO be prepared to articulate your complaint/issue, listen to your manager's side of things, give/receive constructive feedback AND (this is a biggie) be ready to say, "I'm sorry" if the situation calls for it. Any argument or tense situation needs resolution. You should always opt to find a healthy way to end conflict and shift the energy back into a positive direction.

Resolving conflict doesn't have to be a huge ordeal, but it does have to be addressed. It's going to happen. The good news is that with maturity and thoughtfulness, it can be resolved.

Become Empathetic and Sympathetic

Many workers will never know what their supervisor is going through. We all have pressures in life that we have to deal with, but on top of personal pressures, your manager has to deal with bills, inventory costs, payroll, repairs and the list goes on. Not to mention, your supervisor has a lot of pressure coming from corporate to be on top of their game and to make sure they are doing all they can to ensure the success of the brand. Now, this doesn't make their needs more important than yours, but just as you expect your manager to be sympathetic when things happen to you, you should extend that same grace to them. Take time to genuinely stop to ask how they are doing and inquire how you can help them with anything that needs to be handled. We all need grace and love in stressful times in our lives, and as an employee, it shows a lot of strength of character when you freely extend it to others.

Developing a relationship with your supervisor is essential to thriving in the workplace. Don't take for granted this kind of relationship. You'll never know what may flourish as a result of your connection. Go ahead. Connect.

CHAPTER 4: WHAT WOULD YOU DO?

Scenario 1: Your supervisor seems to be hard on you. You feel that you do your work, are on time and give good service. You think your supervisor should have some slack with you because of your performance and you're obviously frustrated. How do you address this issue?

Scenario 2: Your manager really likes you and seems to give you privileges they don't give to others. It has begun to affect the work environment and how your co-workers relate to you. Do you see this as an issue? Do you ignore the obvious tension and keep accepting special favors? Do you say something to your manager and if so, how would you address the situation?

Scenario 3: You notice your supervisor takes a lunch break at the same time as you every day. You both sit in the same area but never speak to each other. It's the same thing every day. How could you capitalize on this moment? Do you see it as an opportunity to get to know your supervisor? How would you break the ice?

CHAPTER 5
THE WOLF

Wolves hunt as a group. Banding together, they stand in a circle, nose to nose and wag their tails. Then they find their prey.

One of the most challenging and rewarding experiences was developing and maintaining healthy relationships with my co-workers. Admittedly, I had a hard time at first because my pride was in the way. I was the 32-year-old guy who had a decent resume, some nice life experience and there I was working around a bunch of "kids" (anybody under 24 was considered young and unrelatable to me). Yeah, I had a pretty arrogant mindset. A friend on Facebook unknowingly helped me when she posted a status in reference to a situation she was experiencing. She wrote, "I hope the high horse you're on gets cataracts and osteoporosis." I had a gut-busting laugh, but also a sobering moment to think about this experience of working in a restaurant and what I wanted to make of it. I needed to get off my high horse. I had to change and it began by forging new relationships with my co-workers, getting to know them and letting them get to know me.

Establishing relationships with your co-workers is essential to thriving in an environment that focuses on teamwork. It will also strengthen you as a person. You will not survive the world of customer service without the support and help of your co-workers. You need each other in order to thrive.

Co-workers, Not Friends

You might have made friends with one of your co-workers and become close to them. Yet, in the work environment you are co-workers, plain and simple. Your outside friendship will try to impact your work relationship and you must not let that happen. I'm not suggesting you don't become friends. Making new friends is what makes life interesting! However, let me share some cautionary tips.

Sometimes you might work in an environment with people you know outside of work. Your manager needs to be assured that your work will not be affected by you working with your friends. My suggestion is to use the advantage of your friendship and make it work for you and not against you. Utilize your communication language, your understanding of each other and make it an asset as you work together.

Work hard to keep your personal relationships from creeping into the work environment. The less people know, the more focused the atmosphere. I've watched a lot of gossip hurt the work atmosphere as people learn about your personal business and it can ruin the focus of other workers. Should you find yourself in a position where you are working with a known friend, your objective should remain to prove that you can be a professional.

As you progress in leadership, it will affect your friendships. As a leader, you cannot show favoritism to your friends. You have a duty to captain the ship by leading and guiding your crew with integrity and honesty. The crew will easily notice if you make your friends do less work, get bigger discounts or take longer lunches. You will have to be strong as a leader and not let your friends walk all over you, but learn how to be firm in your leadership. It's not an easy thing to do, so beware.

Love in the Workplace

Be cautious: Dating at work is a NO NO! Most companies have a non-fraternization policy in place, which means "get caught dating as employees and you can/will be terminated." This is a serious rule companies have put in place to prevent improper relationships between managers/employees and employees themselves.

Now let's say you're hard-headed enough to ignore this rule and date a co-worker. Recognize that many relationships that have developed in the work environment do not last and generally end with disastrous results. I've watched many relationships develop and everything was cute and playful...at first. Then the roller coaster happens. They have a small fight (which impacts their shift), they break-up, hate each other's guts, get back together briefly and finally have a big heated blow-up and can never work on a shift with each other again. It makes a mess for working conditions because everyone has to walk on eggshells around the two parties. Co-workers might be forced to pick sides and everyone is miserable when working. It can become an ugly experience, so don't do it.

At Work, Not School

Sometimes at work, it's easy to feel like you're back in high school. There are the jocks, the mean girls, nerds, the loners and the list goes on. It can be easy finding yourself wanting to fit in with the "in crowd." No one wants to feel alone in any environment. That's understandable.

In the beginning, my co-workers didn't know how to relate to me, but they were intrigued by my persona. Soon, however, my co-workers saw how much fun I was having with the customers and how the energy in the store was changing and they wanted to get in on the fun. That opened the door for better communication and relationships with my co-workers.

I might not have been popular at first and was talked about by the "mean girls," but eventually, by just being myself and doing my job, I set a standard in the store. There were even a couple of my co-workers who tried to emulate my style with the customers and that was really cool and flattering. You can have that same impact. Unlike high school, there is more at stake in the work environment.

Trying to fit in and be like others can negatively impact your work performance, evaluations, raises and might cast you in a negative light among the staff and management. Learning how to stand tall and be you causes you to be a positive influence in the environment, helps your progression on the job and allows you to connect with co-workers and customers in amazing ways.

Watch how people will gravitate to you when you stay true to who you are. They will respect you. They will learn your character, how to respond to you and will draw from your courage to work to be themselves. You may not be invited to hang out or be included in everything and that's okay. You are not at work to be "Mr. /Miss Popular." You'll be noticed by the people who matter and when that happens, you'll be glad you didn't try to fit in.

Conflict Resolution

The same rules of dealing with conflict with your manager apply here. You have to address issues with co-workers. It's easy to blow-off a co-worker thinking, "I don't have to talk to them. I'll just avoid them." While you have the right to do this, you do not want things to fester and possibly blow-up in your face because you haven't dealt with the issue. It may not be easy and you may feel uncomfortable dealing with it, but addressing the problem helps to clear the air and allows everyone to go back to work with productive minds.

You also want to deal with conflict before your manager has to step in. Be mature enough to deal with your own issues. Now if you call your manager in to help mediate the situation, that shows a level of maturity which says you are aware that someone with a more level head needs to help bring resolution to the problem. However, if your manager has to step in because you and your co-worker can't settle things, it shows immaturity on your part and that might not look favorably on you. Handling conflict is a chance for you to show maturity and leadership. You can't expect the other party to be the mature one, but if you step up to work things out it can only show you in a positive light to your peers and manager.

Communication

One of the things that probably frustrated me the most was the way my co-workers talked to each other. The shifts were filled with "What do you want?!" or "You can't tell me what to do!" or "I know what to do!" It was annoying to watch how they communicated with each other. My aunt used to say, "Put a little sugar in your tone," which meant to speak with more pleasantness and sweetness. As a crew member and co-worker you should work hard to speak with your co-workers in positive tones. When making a request, the words "please" and "thank you" go a long way. When asking for clarification, "Excuse me, can you repeat that?" works better than "What you say?!" As co-workers, you all have to learn how to communicate positively and effectively with each other in order for a productive atmosphere to take place.

This is especially important in the tense moments. Every customer service environment has its tense moments, from lunch rushes to holiday sales to special events. It's easy to get overwhelmed and frustrated by the intensity of the moment, demands of the customers and the emergent needs of the store (out of stock item, issues with restroom, electronic issues, etc.). In these moments you need strong, effective communication with your co-workers.

Don't yell, throw things, scream or get mad. If you need assistance, learn how to speak calmly and articulate your needs. Communication, both verbal and nonverbal, is essential to a cohesive working environment and you have a part to play in that equation. Learn how to be a good communicator in any kind of circumstance and you will be respected among your peers and leadership team.

Work vs. Play

My first job at age 15 was in an ice cream shop. My first shift was with a girl named Channel. We were getting along and there was a lull in customers coming in the store. Somehow, we started throwing water at each other playfully. Then she grabbed a towel and playfully hit me. I playfully swatted her arm. She hit me a little harder and I, still playing, pinched her. The playing stopped and I had crossed the line. I recognized the change in Channel's demeanor and knew I messed up. I immediately started apologizing—A LOT. I thought all was well, until the owner called to check on us. He heard that "something's wrong" in Channel's tone and I was in trouble. I didn't lose my job, but I could have. I have learned greatly from that experience.

As a manager, I believe in having fun at work. I never expected for my crew to keep working every minute of every shift. Now I always expected productivity, but sometimes in order to get that productivity, you have to allow the staff to loosen up. If I have learned anything from my first job experience, I learned that there can be too much play at work and that play time can go too far. I made sure to teach my crew how to play, laugh, and joke and how to turn it off. It's important to remember that you are still in a professional working environment and you can't let your play overtake that fact. So, here are a couple things to remember:

You don't have to be a "goody goody" and work every single second. If the crew is engaging in a moment of laughter, join in. It's okay. On the other hand, while you take a moment to laugh, keep your eyes fixed on what's happening in the place, so if a customer needs your assistance or an issue needs tending to, you can break away to do your job. This shows your co-workers that you know how to focus your priorities and that will challenge them to do the same. It will also make you look good in your manager's eyes. You do well to know how to have a little fun, but also know when to turn it off to focus on your work.

Just as you understand how to communicate professionally with your co-workers, you should also learn the rules of "joking" with your co-workers. I once had a pretty tense moment with one of my co-workers, who referred to me jokingly as "big boy." That offended me and I had to teach him that he was not to refer to me that way. Yes it ruined the moment, but I had to set the boundaries. You need to learn what topics, names or even physical activity are off limits with your co-workers and vice versa. If you're going to joke, play and laugh, everyone needs to know the ground rules.

Remember the Golden Rule? "Do unto others as you would have them do unto you." It definitely applies in this case.

You may find yourself having a great moment of laughter with your co-workers and a customer comes in and you don't want to ruin the fun. In those moments, I would try to include the customer in the laughter and bring them into the fun. This allowed us to laugh and play for a little longer, but also welcomes the customer into a friendly atmosphere with fun employees. Sometimes you can make the play work to your advantage.

Having fun at work is essential but it is important to know the difference between play vs. work. As you learn how to be able to switch between the two, you'll connect in new ways with your co-workers. Have fun, but don't lose focus.

Hanging Out

There were nights where the shift was extremely busy and frustrating. Every once in a while to decompress, the crew who worked that shift would go out for dessert or appetizers at a local restaurant. It was during those times the staff would get to vent about their frustrations of the shift and enjoy a moment of relaxation and laughter with each other. The next time when working together, there was a lot more ease and fluidity among the crew.

It's good to have moments where you can go out as a team to bond with each other. You learn more about each other in different settings and you are better able to relate to each other when it's time to work together. You'll develop a new outlook on each other as you take time to connect in new ways. Don't be afraid to hang out when the opportunity arises.

Learn From Each Other

There are always opportunities for your growth and you need to take advantage of each one. Each of your co-workers has something to offer to the environment. Some might be really good with engaging the customers, while others are good with administrative tasks or cleaning procedures. As you watch your co-workers excel in their areas, challenge yourself on how you can emulate their work habits to enhance yours.

On the flip side, others may have insight about you of which you may not be aware. It's a humbling process to learn from others about to how you need to grow. Occasionally, I would have a conversation with some of my co-workers to inquire about their view of me and what they thought I needed to work on. Most of it was insightful information and I took to heart what they had to say. We all need each other to grow and if you are willing to learn from others you will surely grow as a person and as an employee.

CHAPTER 5:
WHAT WOULD
YOU DO?

Scenario 1: It's a madhouse. A rush of customers have entered and business is booming. Your position is on register, but you see a need for help in other areas. You've finished with all the customers on the register. Do you stay locked to your register? Do you see how you can help your co-workers? How would you assist in helping to bring peace and order in the midst of chaos?

Scenario 2: You have become cool with many of the staff and they see you as one to vent and complain to about things happening on the job. You know you are being looked at for a promotion and the gossiping and complaining is a problem for you. You don't want to jeopardize your relationships with your co-workers, but you don't want to jeopardize your promotion. How do you handle this situation? How can you help your co-workers curtail their gossiping and complaining?

Scenario 3: You're working a 12-hour shift which includes closing the store. In the last couple of hours, as the closing team starts to close the store, there is a lot of horseplay between your co-workers. You are tired and focused on cleaning up so you can go home. Yet, the horseplay begins to frustrate and irritate you. How do you handle your emotions? How can you shift the focus back to work without ruining the joy in the atmosphere?

CHAPTER 6
THE BEAR

Bears have learned that by waving and being friendly to humans, they are likely to receive positive responses and sometimes food.

I find joy in conversing with and meeting new people. I was able to excel in relationships with customers because I knew how to relate to them and make them feel wanted when they came in for business. It was an added bonus to be able to talk, entertain and party with the customers. It gave them a great dining experience, and that caused them to come back time and time again. As a result, there was a significant increase in guest surveys which boosted the store score, traffic to the restaurant and positive energy in the atmosphere. I'm not saying all this to boast, but to show that the relationship between you and your customers is a very important one. It is probably the most essential to thriving in the world of customer service. It impacts business, your paycheck and even you as a person. Let's explore how to connect with your customers.

Kindness Is Key

It makes me sad to see people being unkind to each other. I've seen workers berate customers and insult them when they could have simply diffused the situation with a little bit of kindness.

I recently had an experience where I was shopping for shoes. I was only a few weeks out of the hospital and still couldn't bend. The customer service agent looked around and pointed to the measuring tool that was under a bench and proceeded to walk away. She had no interest in helping me until I called her back over. She never asked how I was doing as a customer or was even concerned that I was clearly temporarily disabled. It ruined the whole shopping experience. It takes nothing to be kind to someone. That's what this industry is about—helping others and showing kindness. Spread a little love.

Greet the Customer

The first impression you make on a customer is how you greet and welcome them into your place of business. Say "Hi" or "Welcome" and make it good. Don't offer a wimpy, careless "Hello." No, I'm talking about a booming, enthusiastic, friendly "WELCOME!" A fake, uncaring greeting is like a slap in the face, but a warm, energetic greeting brings a smile to the customer's face and shifts their mood as they enter the store.

Remember: *every customer matters*. You will get customers of all ages, sizes and nationalities, and each one is important. Make sure to pay special attention to the customers with special needs. I rushed to open the door for guests in wheelchairs or on walkers. I would go the gentleman route and make sure to walk elderly women to their table arm in arm. I'd playfully talk them up and eventually I'd end up with "girlfriends" who came back to visit me. It is a big plus if you pay attention to children. Parents love when their children are taken care of and treated with respect. It's important and really cool when you make each customer feel special. When they come into your place of business, they should feel wanted and that they matter.

An enthusiastic "hello" can shift someone's day. I've had multiple experiences where customers would come in looking mean and grumpy. I would boom a "hello" and watch even the toughest looking men break into a smile. You never know how someone is feeling or what they may be going through. Your friendly, positive demeanor can break down their defenses, causing an amazing customer service experience.

WELCOME TO THE JUNGLE!

Greeting the customer is the beginning of the journey of a customer's experience and you want to make sure it starts off right.

Prioritize

When a customer enters the business, they should be your top priority. Whatever you were doing should be put on hold so that you can give your focus to the customers. I've gotten frustrated with some of the crew as they were so busy trying to mop or sweep and let a customer stand in the lobby. I watched one young man tell a customer that he would be with him and proceeded to finish stocking while the customer waited. I told him to stop and serve the customer. After he finished, I counseled him that while I understood he was trying to put away the product, he should have A) stopped immediately to tend to the customer, or B) while he put away the product, continue to engage the customer to make him feel wanted and welcomed (ask about their day, see if they have questions, etc.). In either scenario, the customer is made the focal point and that's all any customer wants to feel.

If no one is around, your job is to stop whatever you are doing and take care of the customer. If it's near the end of your shift, you still have a duty to take care of the customer instead of trying to rush out of the store. It's not about you. It's about the customer—always.

Pay Attention

It is important to pay attention to what the customer is saying both verbally and nonverbally. You will learn how to read the language of the stressed out business person, frustrated parent, happy-go lucky person or the person overwhelmed by their first experience at your place of business. Each customer is speaking to you. You have to interpret what they are saying so you know how to meet their needs.

With the customer that seems in a hurry or frustrated, you might want to keep the pleasantries to a minimum and stay focused on handling their business correctly and promptly. For the customer having a first-time experience, calm your mind and prepare to walk them through the elements of the business. Be ready to answer a lot of questions with this kind of customer, even if it takes a big chunk of your time to help them. For the silly, happy-go lucky customer, just let your hair down and have fun with them. These customers are a breath of fresh air. They want someone to engage them in a fun way as they breathe positive energy into the atmosphere. Laugh it up with them and enjoy the experience of serving them.

Paying attention to the customer is a must. You have to interpret correctly what they are saying and not what you think they need. At the restaurant where I worked, we had several customers with special needs come in as well as a couple of different families who returned each week with a parent/spouse suffering with Alzheimer's. As a staff, we all took time to learn their regular order so when we saw the families walk through the door, we would punch in the order. All the family member had to do was pay and quickly return to their seat. We never knew if their loved one might be agitated that day, so we wanted to make their dining experience as easy as possible.

We had customers come in who were physically disabled and were not looking for us to feel sorry for them. They just wanted to be treated normally and for us to help them have a great dining experience. As one who knows sign language, I really enjoyed engaging with the many deaf customers that came in. They were apprehensive to talk to me at first until they realized I knew how to communicate. That made them smile broadly because they knew they could order without a hassle. I share these stories because these customers taught us how to listen better, which ultimately helped us serve the customer better. When you pay attention to the customer, you give them the customer service experience they were looking for and you strengthen your skills in the process.

You also want to pay attention to what the customer may be having trouble articulating. Sometimes, customers come in trying to handle business and they think they are saying the right thing, but you are having trouble interpreting what they mean. For instance, customers would come in to order a "fruit smoothie" (which is a creamy drink), when they really wanted a "cooler" (which is a fruit slushie). After a couple of mistakes with customers, the staff learned to question the customer and make sure they were ordering the right item. Instead of taking for granted that the customer knew what they wanted, we would politely inquire by explaining the difference between the two drinks to make sure they ordered the right item. It happens all the time. The more intent you are on listening to the customer, the less mistakes you'll make when handling their business. Take time to listen.

Develop an Elevator Speech

An elevator speech is a short summary used to quickly and simply define a profession, product, service, organization, or event and its value proposition. This concept is used often in marketing and business practices, but in the world of customer service, this is the moment where you get to introduce and explain your business to the customer.

In my experience, I began to encounter a range of first-time customers or customers who hadn't patronized the restaurant in a very long time and they felt overwhelmed. As I would explain the menu to them, I found myself having to do it quickly as there were many customers to be served. Ultimately, my explanation of the menu snowballed into something I called the "45-second tour" which was a fun, fast-paced speech introducing customers to the menu. It was meant to make the customer laugh and relax, but it also informed them about the elements of the menu. Having the "tour" in my arsenal proved to be an invaluable tool in helping with customer relations.

Developing your elevator speech will help you with your customers. When they ask, "Can you tell me about this place?" you will be able to teach them about the business through your elevator speech. This helps to ease their mind and they will begin to trust you as their teacher. They will follow your lead in how to make it through their experience. A relaxed customer is more open to suggestions and information. You never know how you'll be able to influence their purchasing choices now that they trust you as teacher.

Developing an elevator speech also helps you learn how to articulate efficiently what you want to say and with practice, it eases your nerves when having to explain things to customers. Get to work on your elevator speech.

Be Honest

This is a tricky one. Let me explain.

You will encounter customers who will ask, "How is...?" or "Would you...?" or "How good is...?" which is their way of getting "the real" about a certain product or service. You have a duty to the company to represent them and the product in the best light, but at the same time you don't want to lie to the customer. I knew of one employee who would cheerfully say, "Everything on our menu is good" and I would get so annoyed with her for not being honest. That's how she chose to answer the customer and it wasn't necessarily wrong. I'm a little different.

Now beware, some customers are baiting you to see if you'll return a negative response of "Ewww, that's nasty!" or "That's worthless. Don't buy that." Sometimes they just want to get a bad reaction out of you and then they might use it against you on a survey or in some other fashion. You must not take the bait. Your responsibility is to be as "positively honest" as you can.

When I would get a question about a certain sandwich or meal on our menu, I would inform the customer, "This sandwich is not my favorite as I don't like that cut of meat. However, it is a popular sandwich." Then I would try to sell the sandwich by describing the myriad of ways other customers had customized the sandwich to their liking. This would steer the customer away from thinking, "Well if he doesn't like it, maybe I shouldn't get it" toward "Oh! I can do all those things to build my sandwich. Hmm, maybe I'll try it."

I've learned how to be honest, but keep the focus on the customer making a purchase. Your manager is watching to see how you handle these kinds of moments with customers. Be honest, but remember you are still an ambassador of the brand and you have to always show the brand in a positive light.

As a side note, in my opinion, it is okay to say, "I am not sure about that. Let me check with my manager." I believe it is better to seek out the information, than to stand in front of customers with mouth open trying to figure out the answer to their question. Being upfront and admitting the truth of what you know or do not know keeps the customer calm. They will get the answer to their questions and realize that you are an efficient worker who made an effort to handle their needs. Being positively honest and upfront with a customer is best.

WELCOME TO THE JUNGLE!

Go the Extra Mile

You can always do a little bit more. Open doors for any and everybody. Help the little kid who is trying to be a big boy/girl and make a purchase on their own or offer to help a customer carry their purchase to their car. Customers love red carpet treatment and there is always an opportunity to roll it out.

Think about the times someone went the extra mile for you while you were shopping or dining. Didn't it make you feel good? Why not do it for someone else? Keep your eyes and ears open for the opportunities to go the extra mile.

Deal With Surprises

Stuff will happen. You need to learn how to be flexible and deal with whatever might happen on your shift. You will encounter kids who knock over display cases while running around the store playing tag. There will be people who have eaten too much and will lose their lunch all over the floor or those who haven't eaten enough and might pass out. There will be the customer who makes a mess in the bathroom (overflowing toilet, dirty diapers, etc.) and you have to clean it up. The list of things you will have to deal with on a shift is endless. Stay calm. Take a deep breath and say "It's okay. I'll take care of it."

The customer brings things to your attention because they believe you know how to handle the situation. Sometimes the customer is nervous or embarrassed and you have to be sensitive to that fact. So, suck it up, roll up your sleeves and handle the situation. You'll be fine.

Mess-Ups

Every customer service employee will make a mistake. You will ring up something wrong, over charge on an item or forget something. It happens, but how you handle it is key.

Do not argue. Customers are likely to become frustrated or even angry about the mess-up. You must not become combative with them using statements like "No, that's not what you said." or "I tried to tell you, but you didn't listen." You are making matters worse. Your response is to apologize for the mess-up (whether you were right or wrong) and offer immediately to correct the situation.

You should want to avoid the customer submitting negative feedback (via survey or website) or complaining to your manager. Apologize and make nice with the customer. Offer them a coupon (if the situation warrants it) so they will return for another visit. Diffuse the situation as best as you can. You don't need the headache of a situation that could easily be handled.

Getting to Know All About You

To be honest, if I could entertain and talk to customers all day (without doing all the other stuff) I'd be a happy man. Meeting customers of all ages has brought me great joy. Some of my favorites were the kids I made special handshakes with, the customers I got to interview and learn about their lives or the ones who gave me a good laugh. Here's what I know. Customers have had enough bad customer service experiences. They want someone who will give them great energy and great service. Evaluate yourself in these areas:

Do you show genuine care toward your customers? I always advise new employees not to ask a customer a question if they don't care to know the answer. If you're going to ask a customer "How was your day?" be prepared as they unfold the good/bad details of their day. Sometimes customers just want to share their good news and sometimes they just need to vent. I remember one gentleman who came in angrily venting about his experience at a trailer rental company. He was really mad and I let him vent for 15 minutes before he even made his order. I ended up paying for his meal to try and be a Good Samaritan. The gentleman sat for two hours in the restaurant trying to cool off. I checked on him often and each time I checked on him, his mood softened more and more. By the time he left, I was able to get a little smile out of him and he was grateful for the kindness. Customers need your kindness and genuine spirit.

Have you actually had a conversation with your customers? You'll meet customers who are first-timers, big family customers, young couples in love or even a group of silly friends. These kind of customers are a simple open invitation for you to connect further and get to know. The more you engage customers the more they get to know and trust you. They will look for you when they come into the establishment. They will talk you up to their friends and family and refer people to the business as a result of their trust in you and your service. You never know what can happen from having a simple conversation with your customers. Go ahead and chat it up.

Have you paid it forward? One of the coolest opportunities on my job were the moments where we would take care of someone's meal or dessert. The customers' mouths would fly open in disbelief, but their hearts were full of gratitude. Often people have never had anyone do something special for them. How can you pay it forward with your customers? How can you show the generosity of the human spirit to your customers? When you take advantage of a moment to be generous towards your customer, they won't forget it and will remember you for your act of kindness. Make a conscious effort to find moments to pay it forward and make your customer's day.

There are other ways to get to know your customers and for them to get to know you, but these are the ways that have worked for me. I challenge you to find the ways that work for you. I'm grateful for the customers who have become friends, the senior ladies who became my "girlfriends," and the kids who stopped by to say "Hi" and would talk my ear off about their day. The relationship between a customer service agent and their customer is extremely important and it will benefit you to learn how to appreciate and respect it.

CHAPTER 6: WHAT WOULD YOU DO?

Scenario 1: It's busy and three customers enter. You are doing your last tasks before clocking out. You notice the customers are waiting to be served, but your co-workers are otherwise engaged and the manager is on a business call. Do you keep finishing your tasks and think "I'm going home?" Do you stop and assist the customers? Do you say something to your co-workers and let them figure it out?

Scenario 2: A customer is frustrated because they aren't allowed to use more than one coupon on their purchase. You know the store's coupon policy and try to explain it to the customers. How can you help calm the customer? Do you use the extra coupon just to satisfy them? Do you alert management and allow them to assist in the situation?

Scenario 3: A big party comes in to eat and your co-workers get frazzled. The party seems like a fun and lively group and they just want to eat. How can you assist in taking care of these customers? How can you make their experience an enjoyable one? How do you motivate your co-workers to give excellent service?

CHAPTER 7
THE BALD EAGLE

Bald eagles learn to fly by practicing with their parents and staying near the nest. Eventually, each eagle must leave the nest and explore the world, flying by themselves.

I wrote this book to be a voice of wisdom and insight from all that I've learned. I hope you have gleaned something. Before we end, allow me to leave you with a few final thoughts.

As a customer service agent, if you give out positivity, you'll always receive it back. I was able to keep a smile on my face because there was always some customer making me laugh with their craziness or making me smile with their words of encouragement. Even on my lowest days where things just weren't going right, I would always get a pick me up from a customer who would return the positive energy they had received from me. It was amazing how my day would turn around. Being positive in the work environment improves your attitude, the environment and customer interaction.

Enjoy this world! The world of customer service has a lot of cool and fun elements. I challenge you to find joy in every day you work. My motto, is "However I begin the day, is how I end." So if I started the day on a super high, I ended it on a super high. When this stayed my priority, the workday flowed better and my energy was in abundance.

Everyone is going to leave the customer service world at some point. I wanted to make sure that when I left that I had done all I could to maintain good character, a strong work ethic and positive energy. I wanted to make sure that my life left an impression on everyone that I encountered.

It's like the words of the song, *"If I can help somebody as I pass along; if I can cheer someone with a song; if I can show someone that he's traveling wrong; then my living shall not be in vain."* That's important to me in all that I do.

I also want to challenge you that when you leave any position from any job, you leave the right way. I've watched too many people leave in a huff on a shift, or not show up for their shift (their way of quitting) or even having to be fired for illegal acts on the job. In any of these circumstances, all that was left of the person's legacy was the manner in which they left. They became the subject of gossip around the workplace. If you want to leave your job, give proper notice, work hard in your last days of work and leave a positive image in the minds of your co-workers and customers.

Think about it. *How do you want to leave your legacy?*

Jonathan J. Johnson

 @Jonathan J. Johnson

 @jjjthewriter

 Johnsonjjonathan@gmail.com

 (734) 219-3983